The 1940s

Britain in Pictures

The 1940s
Britain in Pictures

PA Photos

AMMONITE
PRESS

First Published 2008 by
Ammonite Press
an imprint of AE Publications Ltd,
166 High Street, Lewes, East Sussex BN7 1XU

Text copyright Ammonite Press
Images copyright PA Photos
Copyright in the work Ammonite Press

ISBN 978-1-906672-10-2

British Cataloguing in Publication Data. A catalogue
record of this book is available from the British Library.

Editor: Paul Richardson
Picture research: PA Photos
Design: Gravemaker + Scott

Colour reproduction by GMC Reprographics
Printed by Colorprint, China

Page 2: Charterhouse
Street, Holborn, looking
towards Smithfield, London,
during the Blitz.
10th May, 1941

Page 5: Holiday-makers
enjoy the sun on
Bournemouth beach.
1st July, 1946

Page 6: A family at home
watching television.
15th December, 1949

Introduction

The archives of PA Photos yield a unique insight into Britain's recent past. Thanks to the science of photography we can view the 20th Century more accurately than any that came before, but it is thanks to news photography, and in particular the great news agency that is The Press Association, that we are able now to witness the events that made up life in Britain, not so long ago.

It is easy, looking back, to imagine a past neatly partitioned into clearly defined periods and dominated by landmarks: wars, political upheaval and economic trends. But the archive tells a different story: alongside the major events that constitute formal history are found the smaller things that had equal – if not greater – significance for ordinary people at the time. And while the photographers were working for that moment's news rather than posterity, the camera is an undiscriminating eye that records everything in its view: to modern eyes it is often the backgrounds of these pictures, not their intended subjects, that provide the greatest fascination. Likewise it is revealed that Britain does not pass neatly from one period to another.

The years between 1st January, 1940 and 31st December, 1949 saw the country taken to the brink of disaster, and begin its initially shaky journey to recovery. Unlike the First World War, for Britain the Second was fought as much its cities, towns and villages as it was in Europe and elsewhere – in its skies too, as the pivotal stage of the war known as the Battle of Britain raged in the summer of 1940 and the air war brought the front line to the cities. In no other British war have ordinary people participated so actively as their homes were destroyed, their children evacuated, their lives overturned.

While the second half of the decade is often characterised as an aftermath of that conflict, we see, in the pictures of the time, a looking-forward, not back. The marriage of the young Princess Elizabeth and the birth of her first child Charles meant that by the end of 1949 Britain had a new Royal family in waiting. More ordinary women were also stepping forward: having moved into traditional male roles by wartime necessity, it seemed unlikely that they would entirely settle back into meek domesticity.

Something else had changed. A flickering blue light in the corners of some parlours heralded a new age for news, entertainment and society. Its repercussions for families – Royal and common alike – were to be profound.

King George VI, the Queen
and Princesses Elizabeth
and Margaret take a ride in
the countryside in wartime
Britain.
1940

Cambridge University defeated Oxford University in the 1940 Boat Race. Due to the War this was held at Henley, for the first time since the inaugural Boat Race in 1829.
1940

A motorcyclist of the 1st Canadian Reconnaissance Squadron enjoys a cup of tea during an interlude in the day's work. Behind him can be seen a Lewis machine gun of First World War vintage.

1940

RAF pilots, fighting the air war over occupied France, relax with their mascots on and around a Spitfire.
1940

John Logie Baird, pioneer of
television, demonstrates his
latest invention – for showing
television pictures in full,
natural colours.
1940

Some of the men who answered the British Army's call for volunteers with recruiting Sergeants at a West London recruiting office.
1940

Facing page: London schoolchildren, from heavily-bombed districts, take their treasured belongings to safer quarters.
1940

A female worker in the City still smiling after being rescued from a London building wrecked by a bomb dropped in a daylight Luftwaffe raid.
1940

Winston Churchill at the
Debutantes' Ball, at which
his youngest daughter Mary
was one of the 220 girls who
'came out'.
1940

Recruits for the ATS
(Auxiliary Territorial Service)
are put through three weeks
of intensive training at a
former hotel.
1940

Wartime recycling: East Ham Borough Corporation issued a pamphlet to "encourage the saving of waste materials of all descriptions which are needed for the national war effort. The Corporation undertakes to return all the materials to the industries concerned."
1940

Gordon Richards glances
over his shoulder as his
mount, 'Quartier-Maitre',
passes the post to win the
Lincolnshire Handicap at
Doncaster.
3rd April, 1940

Two Aintree race-goers read
a notice informing punters
of the air raid precautions at
the Spring Meeting.
5th April, 1940

Facing page: Suitably attired
for their new surroundings
in boots and overalls, four
young children evacuated
to North Cadbury Court,
near Yeovil, Somerset, take
a walk around the farm
attached to the estate.
1st May, 1940

Facing page: British soldiers are assisted by the Royal Navy on their return to England after being evacuated from the beaches of Dunkirk, Northern France, in Operation Dynamo. A total of 338,226 soldiers, mostly from the British Expeditionary Force, were rescued between May 19th and June 4th.
4th June, 1940

Mr A V Alexander, First Lord of the Admiralty, shakes hands with the West Ham United players before the League Cup Final against Blackburn Rovers.
8th June, 1940

Members of the LDV (Local Defence Volunteers) are introduced to the workings of a rifle.
22nd June, 1940

Facing page: On 24th August 1940, Central London was bombed for the first time during the Second World War. Incendiaries were dropped by the Luftwaffe, causing huge fires in the City of London.
24th August, 1940

At the height of the Battle of
Britain, Royal Air Force pilots
wait on the airfield for the
instruction to 'scramble'.
1st September, 1940

A telephone operator at work on a London switchboard wearing a steel helmet during an air raid.
1st September, 1940

A London fireman pauses briefly for a cup of tea as he works to clear rubble caused by the bombing of Central London during the autumn of 1940.
9th September, 1940

Facing page: Prime Minister Winston Churchill surveys bomb damage during the London Blitz.
September, 1940

Soldiers from the 9th Bn,
The Devonshire Regiment,
guarding a Luftwaffe
Messerschmitt Bf109E,
which crash-landed following
a Battle of Britain dogfight
near Beachy Head, East
Sussex.
30th September, 1940

A bus lies in a deep crater
in Balham, South London,
following night-time bombing.
14th October, 1940

Householders emerging from the Anderson shelter in which they took refuge while their house was destroyed in bombing.
25th October, 1940

The ruins of Coventry
Cathedral after the medieval
building, and most of the
city's centre, were destroyed
by Luftwaffe bombs during a
single night in the Luftwaffe's
'Baedecker Raids', which
targeted historic sites of little
military significance.
15th November, 1940

A ban on football during periods of Alert was removed and play went on except in cases of imminent danger. Trained observers kept watch: here Mr R G Brown acts as Spotter during a Charlton Athletic v Arsenal match at the Valley.

7th December, 1940

Colonel Chamberlain
inspects the Chislehurst 54th
Battalion of the Kent Home
Guard.
15th December, 1940

Boys from Battersea in
London help with the harvest
on a Buckinghamshire farm
under the supervision of the
Rev. J A Thompson of their
Youth Club.
1941

Children issued with gas masks at a Clerkenwell, North London school as a precaution against gas attack.
1941

Tea-time in the fields of
Essex, where Land Girls
brought extra acres under
cultivation.
1941

Model tanks and troops are
used to illustrate positions as
an officer, using a shillelagh
as a pointer, lectures to young
Ulstermen in military tactics.
1941

A Luftwaffe officer speaks with a British policeman in St. Helier, the capital of the island of Jersey, during the German occupation of the Channel Islands. The Islands were the only part of the British Isles to be invaded by the Germans.
1941

Facing page: The Blitz Spirit: a Londoner is still smiling while recovering the remains of his belongings from the rubble of his bomb-damaged home.
1941

King George VI and Queen
Elizabeth amid bomb
damage at Buckingham
Palace.
1941

Staff of the Sport and
General Press Agency being
paid their wages outside
their wrecked offices after a
German bombing raid.
1941

A scene of devastation after
a bomb fell on a London
subway near the Bank of
England.
11th January, 1941

John Mills, in his uniform
as a Second Lieutenant,
and Miss Hayley Bell at
Marylebone, London, on the
occasion of their marriage
during the actor's leave from
the army.
16th January, 1941

Police Constable Williams
on duty in London.
10th February, 1941

James B Nicholson, the only
pilot of Fighter Command
to be awarded the Victoria
Cross during the Second
World War, chatting with
village schoolchildren at
Ulleskelf, Yorkshire.
11th March, 1941

Joe Louis (R) sends another
Heavyweight to the canvas.
8th April, 1941

King George VI and Queen
Elizabeth visit the bombed
streets of the East End of
London.
23rd April, 1941

Betsy Riddell (R) and Nancy
Smith (L), working on a West
Sussex farm as part of the
Women's Land Army (Land
Girls).
14th July, 1941

Facing page: An air gunner
examines his guns before
setting out on a firing
exercise at an RAF school
of technical training.
27th May, 1941

An RAF fighter pilot wearing his new parachute.
28th August, 1941

Facing page: Robert Yoghill and William Williams, both formerly of Islington, London, evacuated to a farm at Porthcurno, Cornwall.
1st September, 1941

The first two tanks leaving the factory, which are to be sent to the battle fronts of Leningrad, Moscow and Odessa.

22nd September, 1941

Servicemen have a front line view of the game between England and Scotland at Wembley.
4th October, 1941

WAAF flight mechanics
painting the markings
on an aeroplane.
13th December, 1941

British soldiers are put
through training exercises at
a Weapons Training School
in the Southern Command
during the Second World War.
1942

Harold MacMillan
in his office.
1942

Women help in the
construction of Britain's giant
bomber, the Stirling.
1942

Workers of the Women's
Land Army (Land Girls)
with a spaniel during
a lunch break on a farm
in Sevenoaks, Kent.
1942

An RAF Corporal delivers a
lecture on mooring a barrage
balloon.
1942

A Warrant Officer of the
14/20th King's Hussars with
a cooker and food supplies.
1942

A Land Girl takes a lesson
in sheep shearing at
Pyecombe, near Hassocks,
Sussex.
22nd April, 1942

Away from the turmoil of
the Second World War,
King George VI and Queen
Elizabeth walk in a field with
their daughters, Princess
Elizabeth and Princess
Margaret (R).
30th September, 1942

A Sergeant of the Royal Army Service Corps packs a canister, which is to be dropped from an aeroplane. The canisters deliver food, medical supplies, fuel, ammunition or weaponry. **1943**

American entertainer
Bob Hope enjoys a cup
of tea during a visit to his
grandfather.
1943

The procession of clergy
through the ruins of Coventry
after the enthronement of
the Bishop of Coventry, Rt.
Reverend Neville Vincent
Gorton.
20th February, 1943

Ted Drake (R) and George
Male (C) of Arsenal holding
the Football League
South War Cup after the
presentation by the Duchess
of Gloucester. They won the
match against Charlton 7-1.
1st May, 1943

Her Majesty the Queen talking to Corporal Henry Savaria and A B Grant, with his arm in a sling, during a visit to the Church Army Services Club in Marylebone Road, London.
14th May, 1943

Members of the Women's
Land Army (Land Girls) from
various parts of the country,
some with pitchforks over
their shoulders.
1st November, 1943

American soldiers use their jeep to help in the rescue work and fire fighting during the German bombing raids on London.
1944

American soldiers stationed
in the London area help in
the rescue work during a
German raid on the city.
1944

Betty Wood, a former Leeds
factory worker, 'striking up
the Arc', a searchlight.
1944

The two captains, Scotland's
Matt Busby (L) and
England's Stan Cullis (R),
shake hands before the
match, watched by referee
W E Wood (C).
19th February, 1944

A family group taken on Princess Elizabeth's 18th birthday. (Back, L-R) Duke of Gloucester, Princess Alice of Gloucester, Princess Margaret, Princess Mary, Princess Marina, Earl of Harewood. (Front, L-R) Queen Mary, King George VI, Princess Elizabeth and Queen Elizabeth.

21st April, 1944

British women pour a mess
tin of tea for men from an
American convoy heading
for the south coast of
England during the build-up
to the Normandy landings
(D-Day) of June 1944.
1st June, 1944

A British Army Sherman Tank
rumbles down a street on its way
to a south coast port prior to the
Normandy landings of June 1944
(D-Day). The wartime Censor has
obliterated a sign in the background
as well as the tank's unit markings.
1st June, 1944

World Heavyweight
Champion Joe Louis (L)
throws a left at Tommy
Thompson (R) during an
exhibition bout.
1st June, 1944

An RAF pilot chalks up
the score of his Hawker
Typhoon Mk1B aircraft on
the Squadron board.
6th June, 1944

West Indies cricket captain
Learie Constantine
(second R) leads his team
out at Lord's for a match
against England.
16th June, 1944

The Duke of Gloucester
helping with the gathering of
the harvest at his Barnwell
Manor Farm.
29th August, 1944

A woman acting as a warden in Golden Square during a 'gas attack' exercise in West End London.
6th September, 1944

Damage caused by bombs
dropped in Central London
the previous night.
8th September, 1944

The Oval cricket ground
whilst being used as a
prisoner of war camp during
the Second World War.
29th November, 1944

Facing page: Princess
Elizabeth receives vehicle
maintenance instruction on
an Austin 10 Light Utility
Vehicle while serving with
No 1 MTTC at Camberley,
Surrey.
1945

Winston Churchill amongst
the crowds as he tours
his constituency at
Buckhurst Hill.
26th January, 1945

(L-R) Winston Churchill, Franklin D Roosevelt and Josef Stalin with their advisers at Yalta, in the Crimea, where the Allies decided the future of post-Second World War Europe.
12th February, 1945

Smithfield Market, London, soon after the explosion of a German V-2 rocket. One hundred and ten people were killed in the incident, one of the worst tolls from the V-weapons.
8th March, 1945

King George VI (second L)
is introduced to the Chelsea
players before the Football
League (South) Cup Final.
7th April, 1945

Headlines from a week's
(April 29th - May 5th, 1945)
newspapers, during one of
the momentous periods of
the Second World War.
5th May, 1945

VE Day celebrations in the
East End of London, marking
the end of the Second World
War in Europe.
8th May, 1945

Young London residents
celebrate VE Day amidst
the ruins of their homes in
Battersea.
8th May, 1945

Facing page: Huge crowds
at Trafalgar Square in
London celebrate VE Day.
8th May, 1945

Sir Winston Churchill
waves to a waiting crowd
as he leaves the Houses of
Parliament after the news of
the defeat of Nazi Germany.
8th May, 1945

British men, women and
children celebrating VE Day
in the street.
8th May, 1945

During their tour of the East End of London, King George VI and Queen Elizabeth visit Vallence Road, Stepney, which was badly damaged during a German rocket attack.
10th May, 1945

The crowd sitting on the field
of play during the England v
Australia match at Lord's.
21st May, 1945

Tommy Lawton, England
captain, heading the ball in
the French goal area during
a friendly at Wembley.
26th May, 1945

British Military Policemen
prepare to hoist the Union
Jack to receive the official
entry of the British Army into
Berlin, the German capital.
30th May, 1945

Facing page: St. Paul's
Cathedral: work begins to
repair the damage caused
by Luftwaffe bombing raids
on London.
1st June, 1945

Winston Churchill leaving
Westminster Abbey, London,
after the memorial service
for the late Prime Minister
Lloyd George.
1st June, 1945

Lord's officials hold back spectators who tried to force the Grace gates open after being locked out due to the huge interest in the game between England and Australian Services.
14th July, 1945

Facing page: Crowds watch guns parade along Whitehall.
8th June, 1945

Australia captain Lindsay
Hassett (R) talks to England
captain Wally Hammond (L)
before the start of play at
Lord's. England v Australian
Services.
14th July, 1945

The Houses of Parliament
floodlit on VJ day.
15th August, 1945

Crowds in Piccadilly Circus,
London on VJ Day.
15th August, 1945

King George VI with the Queen, Princess Elizabeth and Princess Margaret on the balcony of Buckingham Palace on VJ Day.
15th August, 1945

Lord Louis Mountbatten,
Commander of the Allied
forces in South East Asia,
presides as General Itagaki
of the Japanese Imperial
Army signs the surrender
document in Singapore.
12th September, 1945

Pilots flying over London
on Battle of Britain Day.
15th September, 1945

Battle of Britain heroes on
their way to Westminster
Abbey for a Battle of Britain
Remembrance Service.
16th September, 1945

Facing page: Fifty one
flags of the United Nations
flying outside Central Hall,
Westminster.
10th October, 1945

Group Captain Douglas
Bader (R) drives, watched
by his playing partner Wing
Commander P B Lucas (L).
10th October, 1945

Mr A V Alexander (L), First
Lord of the Admiralty, is
introduced to the Dynamo
Moscow players before
the match against Chelsea
during Dynamo Moscow's
tour of Britain.
13th November, 1945

Fleet Street, London during
a blackout as a result of
several London gas works
striking.
25th November, 1945

Dynamo Moscow goalkeeper
Alexei 'Tiger' Khomich
makes a flying save during
training at Ibrox, the day
before Dynamo's match
against Rangers.
27th November, 1945

Harlequins' C M Horner (with ball) is tackled by Leicester's Tom Berry (C).
1st December, 1945

HMS Maidstone docked at
Portsmouth carrying 400
ex-prisoners of war, many
of whom are survivors from
the Cruiser 'Exeter', sunk
off Java by the Japanese.
Here the 'Exeter' boys give
the thumbs-up to show their
pleasure at being home.
11th December, 1945

A crowd of civilians and servicemen gather to view the notice posted on the gates of Wandsworth Prison in London announcing the execution of John Amery after he admitted treachery.
19th December, 1945

Twelve year old Daphne Philips gleefully eats the first banana to arrive in Britain after the war, given to her by Alderman James Owen JP, Lord Mayor of Bristol, on the quay-side at Portsmouth.
30th December, 1945

A lamplighter on his rounds
on a foggy day in Blackfriars,
London.
31st December, 1945

In Bethnal Green, East London, smiling women queue for the much awaited bananas which have been scarce since the beginning of the Second World War.
1946

Thousands of people
singing 'Auld Lang Syne'
as their battle song, swept
military and civilian police
off their feet as they tried
to gatecrash their way
into Rainbow Corner, the
American Red Cross Club
in Shaftesbury Avenue, as it
closed down.
9th January, 1946

Eighty feet below the surface
of Piccadilly Circus is part
of the underground station
known as 'Aladdin's Cave'
where national art treasures
from the Tate gallery and the
London Museum were stored
at the outbreak of war. Here
the remaining 200 pictures are
taken from the underground
under police guard.
4th February, 1946

A woman working in Britain's
cotton industry.
16th March, 1946

The Heythrop Hunt moving
through the Gloucestershire
village of Bourton-on-the-
Water on the way to meet at
Cold Aston.
26th March, 1946

Mrs Ford (L), with her
daughter, Ann drawing her
Family Allowance at Mount
Pleasant Post Office.
1st April, 1946

St Johns Brigade cadets
rolling bandages in hospital.
5th April, 1946

Members of the Pioneer
Corps at work in Smithfield
Market, following a decision
of the provision section of
the market to remain on
strike.
15th April, 1946

King George VI presents the
FA Cup to Jack Nicholas,
Derby County captain, after
Derby won the match against
Charlton Athletic 4-1.
27th April, 1946

Princess Elizabeth arriving at the Palace Theatre in London to attend the all-star matinee of '1066 And All That'. Group Captain Peter Townsend (in uniform) looks on as Princess Margaret emerges from the car.
7th May, 1946

Facing page: Abyssinian troops arrive in London for the Victory Parade.
2nd May, 1946

Spinsters rally in Trafalgar
Square for pensions at 55.
12th May, 1946

(L-R) Winifred Shotter, McDonald Hobley and Jasmine Bligh during a rehearsal at Alexandra Palace for the return of television following the Second World War.
21st May, 1946

Crowds assembled for the
night-long vigil to see the
Victory Parade in Trafalgar
Square.
7th June, 1946

Facing page: Tanks and
bulldozers leave Admiralty
Arch in London during the
Victory Parade.
8th June, 1946

Crowds pack the Oxford
Street pavements as the
Victory Parade makes its
way from Marble Arch.
8th June, 1946

Huge crowds around
Nelson's Column watch the
fly-over after the Victory
Parade.
8th June, 1946

The scene from the roof of the Shell-Mex Building in London during the Victory Pageant on the Thames.
8th June, 1946

Facing page: A floodlit Buckingham Palace during Victory Day celebrations.
8th June, 1946

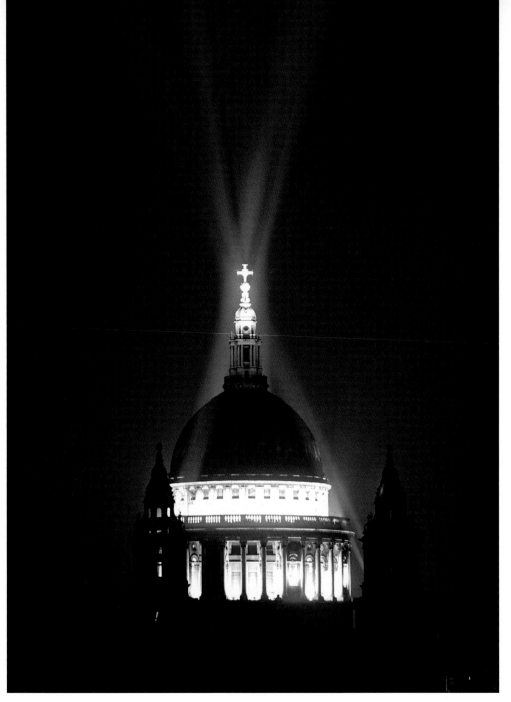

A floodlit St Paul's Cathedral on Victory Night.
8th June, 1946

Facing page: Southampton Docks with 'Queen Mary'.
9th June, 1946

Spectators enjoy a pint
whilst watching England v
India at Lord's.
22nd June, 1946

Facing page: A disabled
ex-serviceman operates
a milling machine.
28th June, 1946

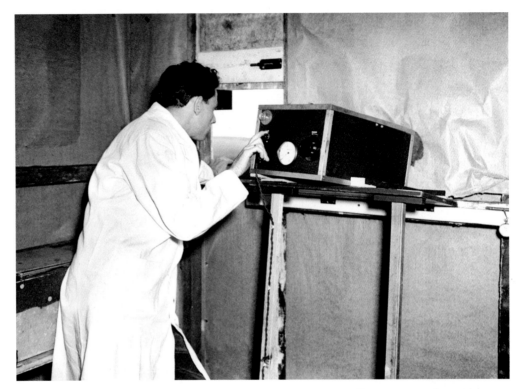

The operator of a prototype shutterless photo-finish camera waits for the runners to pass in front of him during testing. An actual race finish is to be used for the final test before the camera can be installed on racecourses throughout the country.
2nd July, 1946

Facing page: Children on the beach watching a Punch and Judy show.
1st July, 1946

Geoff Brown (R)
congratulates Yvon Petra (L)
on winning the Wimbledon
men's singles tennis final,
the last man to win it wearing
full-length trousers.
5th July, 1946

(L-R front row) Princess Margaret, King George VI, Queen Elizabeth, Group Captain Peter Townsend and Princess Elizabeth, in the Royal Box at the Strand Theatre in London.
5th August, 1946

Facing page: The 85,000 ton 'Queen Elizabeth' occupies almost the entire area of the huge King George V Dock at Southampton. The enormous vessel is being re-fitted from its wartime role as a troop ship to its peacetime role as a luxury cruise ship.
7th August, 1946

Crowds on the beach at Ramsgate.
1st September, 1946

The kitchen of a modern
cottage on display at
the 'Britain can make it'
exhibition at the Victoria and
Albert Museum.
23rd September, 1946

Petticoat Lane, Aldgate,
London.
1st October, 1946

The 83,000 ton Cunard-White Star Liner 'Queen Elizabeth' casts off from her moorings at Southampton to begin her maiden voyage to New York.
16th October, 1946

(L-R) MCC's Major Howard (team manager), Norman Yardley, Wally Hammond and Bill Edrich check to see if the inclement weather has improved. No play was possible on the first day due to the incessant rain. Tour match, Australian XI v Marylebone Cricket Club.
8th November, 1946

A float carrying the FA Cup,
and four of the Derby County
side who won the Cup, rolls
down Lombard Street.
9th November, 1946

Prime Minister Clement
Attlee, Winston Churchill
and other members of
the Cabinet observing
the Two Minute Silence
at the Cenotaph on
Remembrance Day.
10th November, 1946

His Majesty King George
VI and Her Royal Highness
Princess Elizabeth during
the service at the Cenotaph
on Remembrance Sunday.
10th November, 1946

Sweden's Nils Andersson goes on the attack against Bruce Woodcock of Great Britain.
17th December, 1946

A commercial Dakota DC3
lies on top of a house in the
London suburb of Northolt,
Middlesex, after crashing
onto the roof. The plane was
coming in to land at RAF
Northolt when the crash
occurred.
19th December, 1946

A bombed site in the heart
of the City of London with a
poster calling for women to
help in industry.
1947

Princess Elizabeth, Jan
Smuts, King George VI,
Queen Elizabeth and
Princess Margaret.
1947

THIS COLLIERY IS NOW
MANAGED BY THE
NATIONAL
OAL BOARD
N BEHALF OF THE PEOPLE
JANUARY 1ˢᵗ 1947

A sign highlighting
the nationalisation
of the coal industry.
1947

Men clearing snow which
had drifted up to four
feet high, blocking the
Gravesend-Meopham (Kent)
road.
1947

Trafalgar Square, London,
when heavy snow fell in the
city.
6th January, 1947

Mr Mickleburgh, a Bristol
piano merchant, giving away
pianos to be chopped up for
firewood.
31st January, 1947

Chelsea's Harry Medhurst
(L) and Dan Winter (R),
and Charlton Athletic's Bill
Robinson (C), wait for a
cross to come in during a
Division One match.
1st February, 1947

Oliver Hardy scratches the head of Stan Laurel, as the famous pair pose on the 'Queen Elizabeth' at Southampton.
10th February, 1947

Facing page: An ex-servicemen being trained in the forge.
2nd April, 1947

With his score propped against the beer pumps, Mr Victor Cook, landlord of the Park-lane Tavern, Cradley, near Wolverhampton, practises on his bull fiddle while a thirsty customer waits with an empty glass.
7th April, 1947

Charlton Athletic captain
Don Welsh, holding the FA
Cup, and winning goalscorer
Chris Duffy (R, background)
are chaired by their
teammates during the lap
of honour.
26th April, 1947

The courtyard of the
George Inn, Southwark,
where 300 years ago stood
Shakespeare's Globe
Theatre, was the scene of a
presentation in the traditional
Elizabethan manner of 'The
Merry Wives of Windsor'.
26th April, 1947

The shop on the corner of Charlotte Street and Tottenham Court Road in London, where a motorcyclist was shot whilst trying to prevent the escape of three masked men carrying out a raid.
29th April, 1947

Sir Malcolm Campbell sitting
in the cockpit of Bluebird.
1st May, 1947

Reg Parnell, driving a
Maserati 4CL, raises his
hand in celebration as he
takes the chequered flag in
the JCC International Trophy
at Jersey.
8th May, 1947

The Duke and Duchess
of Windsor in the grounds
of Charters.
16th May, 1947

A crowded beach
in Bournemouth as
temperatures soared
into the 80s.
31st May, 1947

HRH Princess Elizabeth,
who drove in a semi-state
Landau from Buckingham
Palace to Guildhall to
receive the Freedom of the
City of London.
11th June, 1947

Actor Laurence Olivier with
his wife Vivien Leigh, in their
London home.
11th June, 1947

Mildred 'Babe' Zaharias
(second R) holds on to the
trophy as she poses with the
runners up after winning the
Ladies' Amateur Open Golf
Championship.
12th June, 1947

Great Britain's Reg Harris (L) crosses the line to win the cycling World Amateur Sprint Championship in Paris.
29th July, 1947

The queue for the Isle of Wight train at Waterloo Station, London.
2nd August, 1947

Famous football internationals (L-R) Stanley Matthews, Stanley Mortensen and George Hardwick taking part in an instructional film being made by the Football Association at Hendon.

17th September, 1947

Mr Eustace Crick, of Melrose
Avenue Cricklewood,
London, yesterday heard
himself publicly described
as 'One Hundred Per Cent'
Husband as he won the
prize at Willesden's Trials.
He is pictured with his wife
and children, Brian and
Angela.
21st September, 1947

England and Middlesex cricketer and Arsenal footballer Denis Compton is massaged by trainer Jack Milne at Highbury Stadium in London.

23rd September, 1947

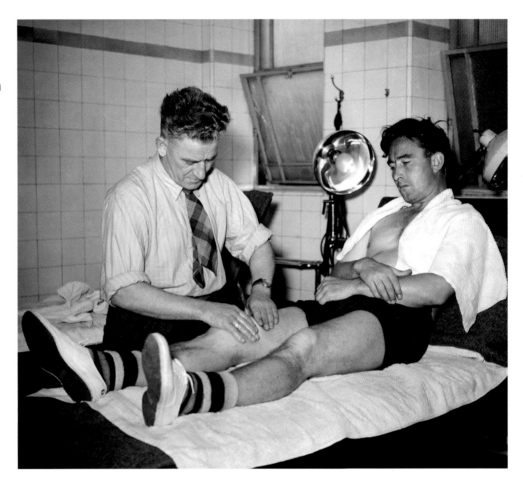

Norman Mighell, Deputy High Commissioner for Australia, and Mrs Mighell give 40 Dr Barnado's emigrants a send off from their Woodford Bridge home as they leave for the SS Ormonde at Tilbery. The boys are to go to a farming school in New South Wales, and the girls to a domestic service training home near Sydney.

7th October, 1947

Members of the Royal
Stables preparing
the Glass State Coach
and the Royal Greys'
harness for the wedding.
9th October, 1947

Princess Elizabeth and Lieutenant Philip Mountbatten, at Clydebank for the launching of the liner 'Caronia', stopped at the Town Hall to receive the town's wedding present – an electric sewing machine.
31st October, 1947

At Stamford Bridge, a
young fan is passed over
the heads of the crowd to a
better viewing position at the
front of the terrace for the
match between Chelsea and
Arsenal.
1st November, 1947

John Shire and Ian Berry
are studying an Official
Souvenir Programme of
the Royal Wedding as they
prepare to sell them along
the procession route.
10th November, 1947

Men helping to construct
a road leading to Wembley
Stadium for next year's
Olympic Games.
11th November, 1947

Buckingham Palace stands
bathed in light against the
night sky as people in their
hundreds surge to the
railings to see Princess
Elizabeth and her fiancé on
the eve of their wedding.
19th November, 1947

Crowds camp out overnight on the streets of London to catch a glimpse of the Royal Couple.
20th November, 1947

The scene at the altar steps during the Royal Wedding ceremony in Westminster Abbey. His Majesty the King stands to the left of the bride. On the bridegroom's right is the groomsman, the Marquess of Milford Haven. The bride's train is held by two pages, Prince William of Gloucester and Prince Michael of Kent.
20th November, 1947

Princess Elizabeth and
the Duke of Edinburgh in
procession to the west door
of Westminster Abbey after
their wedding. Following
are two pages and the eight
bridesmaids.
20th November, 1947

Princess Elizabeth and
the Duke of Edinburgh as
they leave Westminster
Abbey after their marriage
ceremony.
20th November, 1947

Princess Elizabeth and the
Duke of Edinburgh with
their eight bridesmaids
in the Throne Room at
Buckingham Palace, on
their wedding day.
20th November, 1947

Princess Elizabeth enjoys
a stroll with her husband,
The Duke of Edinburgh.
23rd November, 1947

Miner trainees decorating
a Christmas tree at their
hostel.
22nd December, 1947

Christmas dinner in a
caravan.
22nd December, 1947

Winston Churchill visits 'Digger', his white kangaroo at London Zoo. The only albino kangaroo in Europe, Digger was presented to Mr Churchill by the Australian Stockbreeders Association.
3rd January, 1948

An aerial view of the Welsh
Bridge area of Shrewsbury
after serious flooding of the
Severn and Wye rivers.
16th January, 1948

Boxing trainer Nat Seller
tapes Freddie Mills' hands
before a sparring session.
20th January, 1948

The Ireland rugby players
are mobbed by jubilant fans
at the final whistle, after they
held off England 11-10 in the
Five Nations Championship.
14th February, 1948

A bus and several cars with an AA scout rendering assistance at the height of a storm that swept between London and Maidstone.
21st February, 1948

Gold Cup winner 'Cottage Rake' (C), with Aubrey Brabazon in the saddle, is led in by owner Frank Vickerman after victory.
4th March, 1948

Spectators watching the
FA Cup semi final between
Manchester United and
Derby.
13th March, 1948

King George VI and Queen
Elizabeth at Westminster
Abbey Maundy Service.
25th March, 1948

Women in the Lancashire coalfields screening stone, shale and rubbish from the coal as it passes on a conveyor belt from the pithead to awaiting railway wagons.
30th March, 1948

Field Marshal Viscount Montgomery of Alamein, one of the British army commanders of the Second World War, has a word for the BBC after his arrival at Northolt from Berlin. He went to the German capital for talks with Soviet Military Governor Marshal Sokolovsky regarding the tension existing between the allied forces there.

7th April, 1948

Craftsman F Boswell shapes
the bows of tennis racquets
for future Wimbledons, at the
London factory of Lillywhite,
Frowd and Co.
15th April, 1948

Australia's Bill Johnston
bowling at a practice
session during Australia's
tour of England.
17th April, 1948

The engine of the mail train
embedded in the wreckage
of the Glasgow-Euston
Express, a crash in which
20 people lost their lives.
17th April, 1948

Winston Churchill and
Field Marshal Viscount
Montgomery leaving after
the unveiling ceremony
of the Roosevelt statue in
Grosvenor Square, London.
18th April, 1948

Manchester United's Jack Rowley (R) climbs high to power a header goalwards in the FA Cup Final against Blackpool.
24th April, 1948

Manchester United captain
J Carey is carried on the
shoulders of his teammates,
after they won the FA Cup
final against Blackpool.
24th April, 1948

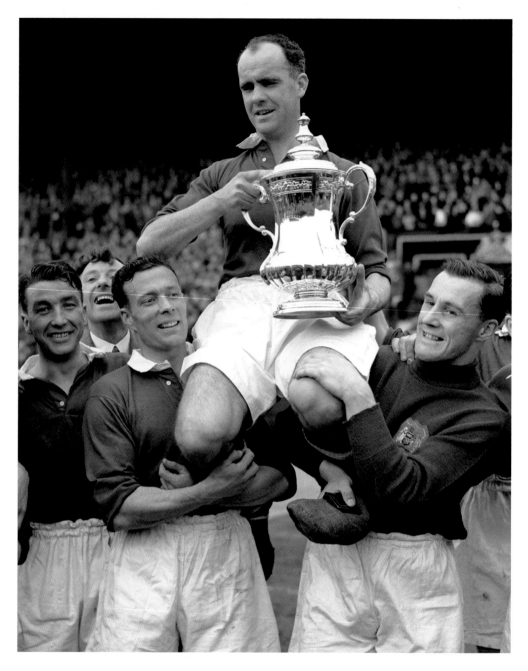

Sir Oswald Mosley
supporters holding an open
air May Day meeting.
1st May, 1948

Windmill Theatre girls
learning the 'can can'
on a roof.
15th May, 1948

Children playing in the sand
at Butlin's Holiday Camp in
Skegness.
1st June, 1948

A man riding a small
motorbike at Ascot
racecourse.
5th June, 1948

A woman having her palm read by a palmist at Royal Ascot.
5th June, 1948

Jamaican immigrants
welcomed by RAF officials
from the Colonial Office after
the ex-troopship 'Empire
Windrush' landed them at
Tilbury.
22nd June, 1948

A couple have fun on
the beach.
1st July, 1948

Performers entertain
local children at Bertram
Mills Circus.
1st July, 1948

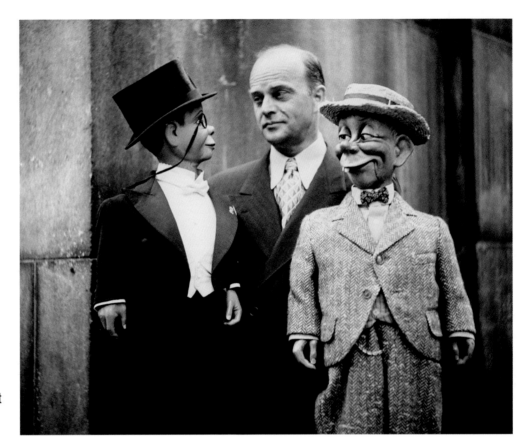

Ventriloquist Edgar Bergen with 'Charlie McCarthy' (top hat) and 'Mortimer Snerd', at the Savoy Hotel, London.
1st July, 1948

Golf Open champion
Henry Cotton makes his
acceptance speech after
collecting the Claret Jug.
2nd July, 1948

John Bromwich (L)
congratulates Bob
Falkenburg (R) on
winning the men's singles
championship at Wimbledon.
2nd July, 1948

Women's Land Army
trainees set out to give
a hand at turning hay in
preparation for stacking.
9th July, 1948

England's Godfrey Evans (L) films the Australia players with a cine camera as they take to the field.
22 July, 1948

A young photographer (L) snaps a picture of Australia's Don Bradman and England's Norman Yardley as they emerge from the pavilion onto the cricket pitch.
22nd July, 1948

Young Michael Setford, sitting on George, the 60 year old giant tortoise at London Zoo.

26th July, 1948

Australia's Don Bradman
makes his way back to the
pavilion through crowds
of well-wishers after helping
his team to victory with
an unbeaten 173 on the
final day of the Ashes
Fourth Test.
27th July, 1948

England captain Norman Yardley (L) congratulates his opposite number, Australia's Don Bradman (R), on his unbeaten 173, which helped Australia set a new Test record by scoring 404 in their second innings to win the game.
27th July, 1948

The British team at Wembley
Stadium during the opening
ceremony of the 1948
Olympic Games.
29th July, 1948

USA's Harrison Dillard
(second L) breaks the tape
to win the men's 100m semi
final at the London Olympic
Games.
30th July, 1948

The photo finish of the final, the first time a photo finish camera was used at the Olympics. USA's Harrison Dillard (bottom) wins gold from USA's Barney Ewell (second from top, silver) and Panama's Lloyd LaBeach (third from top, bronze).
Olympic men's 100m final.
31st July, 1948

The medallists in the men's 100m stand to attention as the national anthem of the winner is played: (L-R) Panama's Lloyd LaBeach (bronze), USA's Harrison Dillard (gold) and USA's Barney Ewell (silver).
31st July, 1948

In the Olympic women's
long jump, Hungary's Olga
Gyarmati leaps to win gold
with a jump of 5.695m.
4th August, 1948

The runners in the Olympic marathon make their way down Wembley Way away from the stadium.
6th August, 1948

Jamaica's Arthur Wint takes over the baton to run the last leg in the Olympic men's 4 x 400m relay.
6th August, 1948

Holland's Fanny Blankers-Koen (R) sprints away to win gold from Great Britain's Audrey Williamson (723) and USA's Audrey Patterson (707) in the Olympic women's 200m final.
7th August, 1948

Argentina's Pascual Perez (R), who was shorn of his long hair by teammates when it was thought he was slightly over the weight limit (an unnecessary precaution as the scales were discovered to be slightly out), steps back after flooring South Africa's J Williams in their third round bout. Perez went on to win the flyweight division Olympic gold medal.
10th August, 1948

'Manny' Shinwell, War Secretary, sees off 1,500 officers and men of the 2nd Guards Brigade from Ocean Dock in Southampton, on their way to Malaya in the 'Empire Trooper'.
5th September, 1948

Aircraft flying over Nelson's
Column in Trafalgar Square
during the 'Battle of Britain'
fly-past, part of the annual
celebration of the air victory
achieved in 1940.
15th September, 1948

Facing page: The beach,
Southend-on-Sea.
6th September, 1948

Two races were won by the King's horses at Ascot. Here is one of the two winners, 'Young Entry', Edgar Britt in the saddle, being led in after the filly's win.

8th October, 1948

Student Gwen Sayers of Coventry learns the technique of cleaning and repairing a fireplace at the National Institute of Houseworkers' training centre at Croydon, London.
12th October, 1948

Julie Andrews, 13 year old coloratura soprano, of Walton-On-Thames, is the youngest star chosen for the Royal Command Variety Performance at the Palladium.
14th October, 1948

Railway lines are strewn with wreckage after a train from Charing Cross to Dartford ran into the back of a Cannon Street to Gravesend train, standing in Woolwich Arsenal Station, London. Two people were killed, and two were injured.
18th November, 1948

A policeman on the
Embankment, London.
27th November, 1948

The engine driver of the 'Queen Mary' boat train receives last minute instructions from the supervisor at Waterloo Station, before setting off on his foggy journey to Southampton.
30th November, 1948

Father Christmas distributes
presents.
8th December, 1948

Princess Elizabeth holds
her baby son, Prince
Charles, after his christening
ceremony in Buckingham
Palace.
15th December, 1948

The radio and stage comedian Arthur Askey at the microphone at the EMI studios in Abbey Road.
24th January, 1949

Girls playing in Regent's
Park, London.
1st February, 1949

Dickens' lovers went along to
The George Inn, Southwark,
to watch scenes from 'A Tale
of Two Cities' presented
by the Dickensian Tabard
Players. The occasion was
the 137th anniversary of
Charles Dickens' birth.
12th February, 1949

Shoppers at Selfridges store selecting their wants from the underwear department, at the end of clothes rationing.
15th March, 1949

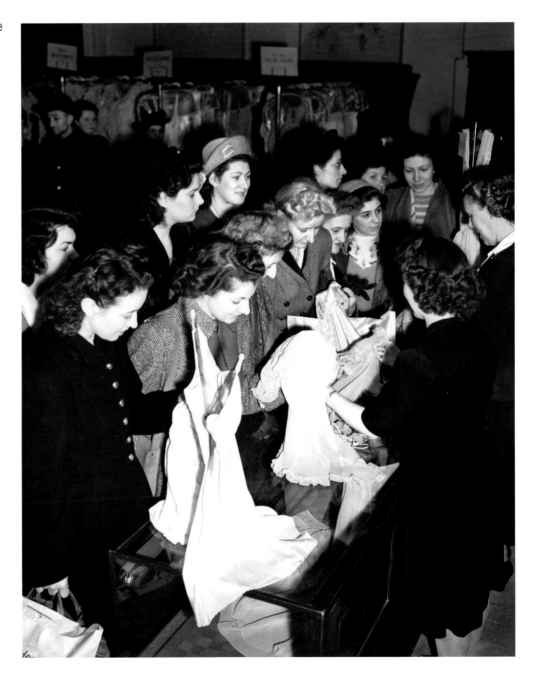

'Russian Hero', with Leo
McMorrow in the saddle,
is led in after winning the
Grand National.
26th March, 1949

Ernest Bevin, Foreign Secretary, signing the North Atlantic Pact on behalf of Britain, in the auditorium of the United States Department in Washington. Looking on is Sir Oliver Franks (L), British Ambassador to the US.

4th April, 1949

Electric signs light up
Piccadilly Circus for
the first time since
the Second World War.
4th April, 1949

Sir Stafford Cripps,
Chancellor of the Exchequer,
waves the famous despatch
case as he leaves 11
Downing Street for the
House of Commons to
present his budget.
6th April, 1949

Motorists on a Surrey road
hailing an AA mobile office.
6th April, 1949

Scotland captain George Young is rushed off the pitch by a policeman after his team won 3-1 against England.
9th April, 1949

Scotland supporters on a
London bus celebrating with
rattles after their team's 3-1
victory over England.
9th April, 1949

The American comedian
Danny Kaye photographed in
his London hotel with
a roll of film draped round
his neck.
19th April, 1949

Leicester City fans in London
for the FA Cup final.
30th April, 1949

In the FA Cup final, Wolverhampton Wanderers' Billy Wright (L), Terry Springthorpe (second L) and goalkeeper Bert Williams (R) can't prevent the ball from going in the back of the net. Leicester City's Ken Chisholm (C) looks on.
30th April, 1949

Princess Elizabeth presents
the FA Cup to Billy Wright,
captain of Wolverhampton
Wanderers, after they
defeated Leicester City by
three goals to one in the final
at Wembley Stadium.
30th April, 1949

Two policemen try to decide
what to do with a swan that
will not move from the road.
1st May, 1949

Actress Honor Blackman,
aged 23, on a motorcycle in
Hyde Park, London.
9th May, 1949

The Royal Engineers
defusing a 2,500 pound high
explosive bomb found in
Dagenham, Essex.
21st May, 1949

Mr Herbert Sparkes, who
is alone responsible for
servicing and running what
is claimed to be the smallest
gasworks in the British Isles.
25th May, 1949

A victorious Bruce
Woodcock (CL) after winning
the British Heavyweight title
in the 14th round against
Freddie Mills.
2nd June, 1949

Arthur Wint, the West Indian runner, getting away to a good start for the 440 yards at the British Games at White City. He won and broke the British record.
6th June, 1949

Making cathode ray tubes
at the EMI factory.
8th June, 1949

Susan has her cup filled at
the Chimpanzees' Tea Party
at London Zoo.
13th June, 1949

Watched by thousands of
spectators, members of the
Haemus Lodge (Brighton
and Worthing District of
Sussex) of the Ancient
Order of Druids conduct
their annual mid-summer
ceremony within the stone
circle at Stonehenge,
Salisbury Plain, Wiltshire.
20th June, 1949

A line of cars waiting to be
loaded during the London
dock strike.
15th July, 1949

A crowd listening to
speakers in Trafalgar Square
during the dockers' mass
meeting.
17th July, 1949

One of the crew pulls in a
parent swan with a hook, to
determine ownership during
swan upping on the Thames.
20th July, 1949

Sorting blanks for die
stamping of sovereigns at
the Royal Mint.
21st July, 1949

Donald Campbell sits in his
father Malcolm's 'Bluebird'
hydroplane, the boat he will
use for an attempt on the
world water speed record.
22nd July, 1949

Brian Close, the youngest
ever player to represent
England in a Test match,
bowling on his debut against
New Zealand.
23rd July, 1949

Wearing his picturesque uniform as Bargemaster to the Fishmongers Company and assisted by a megaphone, Mr Harry Phelps starts the 235th race of the Thames Watermen for Doggett's Coat and Badge at London Bridge.
29th July, 1949

Facing page: A crowd gather to read the notices posted on the doors of Wandsworth Prison, London, following the execution of John George Haigh, 39, for the murder of Mrs Olivia Durand-Deacon, a 69 year old Kensington widow.
10th August, 1949

HMS 'Amethyst' about to
come alongside the quay at
Hong Kong Naval Dockyard.
10th August, 1949

Ballet dancer Anton Dolin, flexing his muscles on the terrace of his London home after flying back from Cannes, where he had been beaten up and robbed at the hands of a notorious Riviera bandit whom the French police had been hunting for two years. Dolin was able to identify him, leading to his arrest.

20th August, 1949

Film stars Stewart Granger
and Jean Simmons watching
the boxing at Harringay
Arena, London.
6th September, 1949

Men of the Thames Police
rehearsing for the pageant
they are presenting to
commemorate the 150th
anniversary of their force.
8th September, 1949

Foreign Minister Ernest
Bevin arrives back at
Southampton after talks in
Washington. Bevin waves his
hat in cheerful response to
dock workers' cries of 'Good
old Ernie'.
12th October, 1949

(L-R) Jockeys Lester Piggott
and K Southwell.
27th October, 1949

One of the greatest
welcomes ever accorded a
ship's company was given
to the 150 sailors from the
frigate HMS 'Amethyst' when
she docked at Devonport,
Plymouth, at the end of her
10,000 mile voyage. Here
the ship's company march
through the crowded streets
of the city.
1st November, 1949

Comedian Michael Bentine,
29, rehearsing his act two
days before his appearance
at the Royal Command
Performance, to be held at
the London Coliseum.
5th November, 1949

Comedian Bob Monkhouse and his bride Elizabeth Thompson at their wedding reception at Caxton Hall, London. Harold Berens is taking a bite of their cake as they attempt to cut it.

5th November, 1949

Towering above the King George V dry dock at Southampton is the gigantic hull of the Cunard-White Star liner 'Queen Mary' as she undergoes a six week overhaul and renovation.
10th November, 1949

The Prince of Wales on his
first birthday, being driven
from Marlborough House,
London after visiting his
great-grandmother Queen
Mary.
14th November, 1949

14-year-old show jumper
Pat Moss jumps her pony
over her 20-year-old brother
Stirling Moss' racing car at
their father's farm at Bray,
Berkshire.
19th November, 1949

Arthur English plays pepper
pot draughts with Windmill
girl Madeleine Hearne,
watched by Irene King and
Beryl Catlin, in the canteen
of the Windmill Theatre,
London.
27th November, 1949

Heads and bodies are buried
in the scrum of the Eton Wall
Game.
30th November, 1949

Audrey Hepburn, principle
dancer in 'Sauce Tartare',
makes friends with a macaw.
1st December, 1949

Television announcer Sylvia
Peters before a television
camera.
8th December, 1949

The Publishers gratefully acknowledge PA Photos, from whose extensive archive the photographs in this book have been selected. Personal copies of the photographs in this book, and many others, may be ordered online at www.prints.paphotos.com

AMMONITE
PRESS

For more information, please contact:

Ammonite Press

AE Publications Ltd. 166 High Street, Lewes, East Sussex, BN7 1XU, United Kingdom

Tel: 01273 488005 Fax: 01273 402866

www.ae-publications.com